Picture credits
T=top B=bottom M=middle L=left R=right C=centre

6-7C Franc Podgorsek/shutterstock; 7C Scott Maxwell/shutterstock; 7B Wong Sei Hoo/shutterstock;
10B Paul Almasy/CORBIS; 13L Joyce Sherwin/shutterstock; 14-15C Wendy Kaveney Photography/shutterstock;
17T ann triling/shutterstock; 22C Haji Saifulbahar Bin Haji Ya'acob; 23T Danish Khan/shutterstock;
28B Ilya D. Gridnev/shutterstock; 29B Tamara Kulikova/shutterstock; 30B Jared Hudson/shutterstock;
31T Neven Mendrila/shutterstock; 31B Alex Melnick/shutterstock; 32L Gianni Giansanti/Immaginazione/Corbis;
32-33C zastavkin/shutterstock; 35T Carsten Medom Madsen/shutterstock; 38C Haji Saifulbahar Bin Haji Ya'acob;
39B Danish Khan/shutterstock; 40L Kampanat Chittithaworn; 41R Kampanat Chittithaworn;
43T ARTEKI/shutterstock; 45T John Van Hasselt/shutterstock; 45C Radu Razvan/shutterstock;
illustrations by Q2A media.

© Really Useful Map Company (HK) Ltd.
Published by Robert Frederick Ltd.
4 North Parade Bath, England.

First Published: 2006

Designed and packaged by
Q2A MEDIA
Printed in China.

RELIGIONS
Contents

THE BEGINNINGS OF RELIGION

Early man noticed forces in nature that were beyond his control but affected him. In order to understand what was behind these forces, man first came up with the concept of a god. The people then thought there were different forces behind each natural event. From this came the idea that there were many gods – a god of the air, a god of the seas, a god of good and one of evil and so on.

WHAT IS RELIGION ?

Religion is a set of rules for living which are usually based on the teachings of one or more spiritual leaders. Most religions also include a belief in a supernatural power or powers that created the world and govern it. A religion may be personal, that is rules followed by one person. But generally religion refers to a set of beliefs that are followed by many people. The major religions of the world are each followed by many millions of people.

✠ *The horned cap believed to have been worn by the ancient Sumerian god of wind, Enlil*

ANCIENT RELIGIONS

Early people had religions that talked about many gods in order to explain the world around them. A religion that believes in many gods is called polytheism. The religions of ancient Egyptians, Africans, Chinese, Sumerians, Greeks, Romans, Norse and many others had many gods. The concept of a single god was first born over three thousands years ago. This was put forth by the ancient Egyptians. The people of ancient Egypt developed the idea that there was actually only one god who might have helpers in the form of lesser gods or even angels. Such a religion is said to be monotheistic.

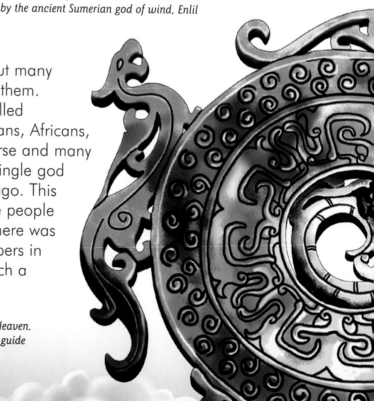

✠ *Ancient Chinese considered jade the Stone of Heaven. Jade pi discs such as this one were believed to guide the soul of a dead person to heaven*

A CHRONOLOGY OF RELIGIONS

Judaism was the first modern world religion to believe in a single god – about 3,000 years ago. At around the same time, Zoroastrianism, which was also a popular religion in West Asia, spread the idea that there were two gods, one of good and the other evil. Five hundred years later, religions such as Buddhism, Confucianism and Taoism, which dwelt more on the rules of living a good life and less on the existence of an all powerful God, came into existence. Then, about 2,000 years ago, came Christianity, which is the world's largest religion today. It was followed 700 years later by the world's second largest religion, Islam. About 500 years ago Sikhism, which combined the elements of both Hinduism, a polytheistic religion, and Islam, a monotheistic one, was born. About 160 years ago came Bah'aism, a religion which includes ideas from many of the world's religions and emphasises the oneness of mankind.

Christians use rosary beads while chanting their prayers. The rosary is actually a set of prayers dedicated to the Virgin Mary

Driedel, the four-sided spinning top used to play a game during the Jewish festival of Hanukkah. The top has the words Nun, Gimel, Hay and Shin on each side. These letters are said to form the Yiddish phrase Nes Gadol Hayah Sham, meaning "A great miracle happened here"

Buddhist prayer wheels have mantras, or prayers written upon them. Tibetan Buddhists believe that spinning these wheels are just as powerful as chanting the mantras

7

ANCIENT RELIGIONS OF EUROPE

The religions of ancient Europe had many gods, like all other religions elsewhere at that time. There were gods for the sky, water, fertility, love and many other things. There were good gods and evil ones. Most ancient European gods did both good and bad deeds. This is unlike the god of a monotheistic religion in which the god is incapable of evil.

GREEK GODS

The Greeks created many stories about their gods. The Greek gods were said to indulge in all kinds of quite ungodly activities. For example, they plotted against each other, and were married to one god but had children by another god. The main Greek god, Zeus became king of the gods only after many plots and fighting. The Greeks had priests who claimed to communicate with the gods and therefore acted as mediators between the gods and man. The Greeks believed in life after death and thought that good souls went to the kingdom of the Blessed and the bad souls were punished in Hades. Heroes such as Hercules, however, were sent to a special place of bliss called the Elysian Fields.

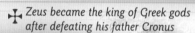
✠ *Zeus became the king of Greek gods after defeating his father Cronus*

✠ *Unlike his Greek counterpart Cronus, Saturn was widely worshipped in Rome. Ancient Romans even built a temple in his honour*

ROMAN ADAPTATION

Roman religion was similar to Greek religion. Like the Greeks, the Romans had different gods for different parts of nature as well as for different functions like love, marriage and health. The Roman gods were, however, more powerful and spiteful than the Greek gods. At first the Romans and Greeks had quite different gods. Later on, as Romans and Greeks interacted with one another, the Romans came to admire the Greek way of life and adopted the Greek gods as their own. The Romans also worshipped their Emperors later in their history.

GREEK AND ROMAN GODS

Title	Greek	Roman
The King	Zeus	Jupiter
The Queen	Hera	Juno
Youth, healing	Apollo	Apollo
War	Ares	Mars
Time	Cronus	Saturn
Sea	Poseidon	Neptune
Love	Eros	Cupid
Hell	Hades	Pluto
Hunting	Artemis	Diana
Wisdom	Athena	Minerva
Agriculture	Demeter	Ceres
Messenger of the Gods	Hermes	Mercury

NORSE GODS

The ancient people of Scandinavia called the father of all the other gods Ymir. Ymir was a giant who was fed by a cow. This cow made a man by licking a salty block of ice. From this man came the king of gods, Odin and his brothers. Odin killed Ymir and created the world from the giant's body. Ymir's flesh became the earth, his bones became the mountains, and his blood became the oceans. Odin and his brothers also made the first man and woman from two pieces of driftwood. Odin was the most powerful Norse god. Tyr and Freya and Thor were the other main gods in Norse mythology and were Odin's children.

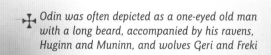

✠ *Odin was often depicted as a one-eyed old man with a long beard, accompanied by his ravens, Huginn and Muninn, and wolves Geri and Freki*

✠ *Audumla, the sacred cow licking the ice-covered body of the Frost giant Ymir, to create Buri, Odin's grandfather*

9

THE RELIGIONS OF AFRICA

Africa is a huge continent with a vast number of different peoples and tribes. Almost every tribe had its own gods and beliefs. Although the majority of Africans are either Christians or Muslims today, many still follow the traditional religions that they have followed for thousands of years.

ANCIENT EGYPT

The ancient Egyptians were polytheistic. Egyptian worship included the sacrifice of animals and processions. Ancient Egyptians believed that the soul went to a new world, just like this one, so, the grave of a dead person should contain everything that person might need in the next world. It was in Egypt, however, that people first started moving towards monotheism – the idea of just one god. The idea was promoted by the Pharaoh, Akhenaten. He started the worship of the god Aten and encouraged his people to believe that Aten was the only real god. After Akhenaten died, however, the Egyptians went back to worshipping their many gods.

✝ *Witch doctors claim to be able to expose evil magicians and witches*

MAGIC AND WITCH DOCTORS

Magic is a common factor in most African religions. There are good magicians who make amulets and charms to protect their wearers, and there are evil magicians who make potions and poisons to harm people. A kind of magic called divination is also used to foretell the future. Many Africans also believe in witches who feed on the souls of living people making them fall sick and die.

SPIRITS OF THE EARTH

Many Africans worship what they believe to be the spirits of the Earth. The Ashanti tribe of Ghana believe in Asase Yaa, otherwise known as Mother Thursday. Therefore, these people do not work in the fields on Thursday. In temples in Nigeria the Igbo people worship the Earth goddess Ala who is portrayed as carrying a child in her arms similar to the Madonna. The people of Benin believe in Olokun, the god of the sea. He is thought to be a king who lives in a palace under the sea, just like Poseidon, the Greek god of the sea.

✠ *Many African tribes continue to worship the Earth*

✠ *The chief gods of the ancient Egyptians – Seth, Horus, Isis, Osiris and Anubis*

✠ *Ancient African tribes wore amulets and charms to protect themselves from evil*

WORSHIPPING THE DEAD

Many religions of the world encourage prayers to the dead and some even worship the dead. In East and South Africa worship of the dead is particularly strong. The dead are often represented in the form of death masks. The Ashanti, Zulu and Swazi people also worship great kings of the past.

GODS OF THE FOREST

THE PYGMIES who live in the forests of Africa believe in the **GOD OF THE FOREST.**

This is a good god who is often worshipped with the offering of a basket of fruits.

These people have many joyous songs about the forest god and there are many rituals that involve dancing and feasting in honour of this god.

11

NATIVE RELIGIONS

Ancient religions of native tribes were mainly based on nature. Each tribe had its own set of beliefs and rituals. However, some of the common beliefs included shamanism, animism and faith in the Supreme Being. Today, religions of many tribes, such as the Australian aboriginals and Native Americans are almost lost as more and more people adopt Christianity.

ANIMISM

The term animism refers to the belief that "all objects, living or non-living, have a soul". Animists therefore treat everything around them, including plants, animals, rivers, and all forces of nature with utmost respect. Animism promotes the belief in spirits. Some Native American tribes believe that the spirit of a person remains on the earth as a ghost. The Aborigines of Australia were also deeply influenced by animistic beliefs. According to Aboriginal mythology, the spirits of their ancestors inhabited the earth at the beginning of time. It was only later that the sky-god created man and all other living beings. Animism is responsible for the faith in shamans and has also contributed to animal worship.

✝ *Aborigines believe that the world was created during a period called Dreamtime*

SHAMANISM

Shamanism was not exclusive to Native American religions. However, shamans played a very important role in the Native American society. A Native American shaman was believed to have the powers to communicate with the dead and heal the sick. They were also thought to cross over from this world into the world of spirits and speak to the souls of the dead on behalf of their relatives and friends. Every Native American tribe had its own shaman. Only those who "received the call", man or woman, could become a shaman.

✝ *Shamans are healers or spiritual leaders who practice magic and act as mediums between the visible world and the invisible spirit world*

✝ *All Native American tribes believed in the 'totem', an animal or object that is said to protect a particular tribe or person. Totems of each tribe were often carved on decorative wooden poles and placed in the centre of the village*

12

ROLE OF ANIMALS

Animals play a vital role in the Native American culture. The Coyote was the most prominent animal in Native American myths. Sometimes he was seen as a hero, while on other occasions he was portrayed as an evil spirit. Other important animal figures in Native American culture are the Raven and the Rabbit. Some tribes even worshipped the serpent. Quetzalcoatl, the chief God of the Mayas and Aztecs was portrayed as a winged serpent. The Aborigines also worshipped animals. According to one Aboriginal tribe, two brothers, known as the Bagadjimbiri twins, emerged from the ground in the form of dingoes to create the world.

MANY GODS

Most Native American tribes believed in one Creator God who had no form. A mythical hero or trickster animal like the coyote represented this God on earth and taught man culture and etiquette. Apart from these, the Native Americans believed in spirits that controlled the weather and ruled the underworld. The Australian Aborigines also believed in many gods and spirits. Each tribe believed in a sky god who was the Supreme Being. The spirits of Aboriginal ancestors were thought to have served this god. Many of the lesser gods, or helpers of the sky god, were portrayed as animals, especially the serpent.

ABORIGINAL SOLAR DEITIES

GNOWEE
this goddess was believed to carry a torch and climb up and down the sky everyday in search of her lost son

WURIUPRANIL
was thought to walk across the sky, from east to west with a torch in her hand, dipping in the ocean in the west

YHI
a Dreamtime goddess who was awakened from her sleep by a whistle. Light fell on the world when she opened her eyes

WALO
used to walk across the sky with her sister Bara, until one day she realised their combined heat was scorching the Earth. Then on she walked across the sky alone

SEVEN SACRED RITES OF THE LAKOTA NATIVE AMERICANS

Sweat Lodge: a purification rite in which the person sits in an enclosure containing fire. The heat from the fire is thought to cleanse the person of guilt and sins, bringing him closer to the Wakan Tanka, or Great Spirit

Vision Quest: carried out by young boys entering adulthood. During this rite the boy observes a certain period of fast and prayer to hear the "voice of the sacred"

Keeping of the Soul: done so that the soul of the dead can rest in peace

Sun Dance: a group of Lakota people dance around a sacred tree looking at the sun. This is done for the good of the future generations

Making Relatives: Sharing of sacred food and pipe in order to strengthen the bond within the tribe

Puberty Ceremony: preparing a young girl for womanhood and childbirth

Throwing the Ball: this rite was performed only by women. The participants tried to catch a ball containing buffalo hair to receive great blessing

13

JUDAISM

Judaism is around 3500 years old and is the oldest monotheistic religion. Christianity and Islam, the two largest religions in the world, both have their origins in Judaism. The followers of Judaism are called Jews. There are about 15 million Jews in the world.

CHILDREN OF ISRAEL

Jews are believed to be the direct descendants of Abraham through his son Isaac and grandson, Jacob. It is said that God promised Abraham, who was childless, a "great nation" filled with his descendants. God then told him to leave the city of Ur in Mesopotamia. Abraham obeyed God's command and set out in search of God's land. His wife Sarah and nephew, Lot also joined Abraham in his journey. After travelling for several years, Abraham and his people settled in Canaan. It was here that Sarah, 90 years old at the time, gave birth to Abraham's son Isaac. Later, Isaac had two sons — Esau and Jacob. The latter was given the name Israel, after he wrestled with God. Israel had 12 children, who founded the Twelve Tribes of Israel. All Jews are believed to be the Children of Israel.

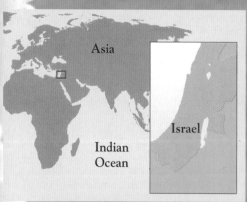

Asia

Israel

Indian
Ocean

✢ Canaan, where Abraham and his people lived briefly, was located near present-day Israel and included the West Bank and parts of Jordan, Syria and Lebanon

✢ The menorah is the oldest symbol of the Jewish religion. It is said that after a successful Jewish revolt against the Greeks, the Jewish army wanted to rededicate the Temple in Jerusalem. However, they only found enough pure oil to light the menorah for one day. Miraculously, the menorah burned for eight days, until more pure oil could be found. During Hanukkah, the menorah is lit to commemorate this miracle

THE STORY OF MOSES

Moses, the prophet, was another important figure in Judaism. He was born into the tribe of Levi. However, his parents abandoned Moses when he was a baby, as the Pharaoh of Egypt had ordered all newborn Israeli boys to be killed. The Pharaoh's sister saw the abandoned baby and took him under her care. Years later, Moses found out about his true identity and dedicated his life to saving his people from slavery. With the help of God, Moses managed to free his people and led them out of Egypt to Mount Sinai. It was at Mount Sinai that Moses received the Ten Commandments from God.

THE JEWISH LAWS

The Torah is the most important document of the Jews. It consists of the first five books of the Tanakh, or Hebrew Bible. The term 'torah' means law in Hebrew. It is also known as the Five Books of Moses, as it was believed to have been written by the great prophet. The Torah tells the story of origin of Judaism and also contains laws for daily life.

✠ *Orthodox Jews would never leave home without the kippah, or skull cap, and tefilin – a small leather box with passages from the Torah inside it*

TYPES OF JEWS

Judaism, especially in Israel has many different groups and sects. The three main groups are Orthodox, Reform and Conservative. Orthodox Jews follow the religion in the strictest way possible. Conservative Jews follow most traditional practices, but less strictly than the Orthodox. Reform Jews are the least traditional of all Jewish sects.

THE TEN COMMANDMENTS

1. I am the Lord your God and you shall have no other gods before me
2. You shall not worship any idols
3. You shall not take the name of the Lord your God in vain
4. Remember the Sabbath day and keep it holy
5. Honour your father and your mother
6. You shall not kill
7. You shall not commit adultery
8. You shall not steal
9. You shall not bear false witness against your neighbour
10. You shall not covet your neighbour's goods

JEWISH HOLIDAYS

Pesach or Passover: celebrates the Exodus from Egypt

Rosh Hashanah: also called the Jewish New Year because it celebrates the day that the world was created

Yom Kippur: a day of penance for sins committed the previous year

Hanukkah: the festival of lights. It coincides with Christmas

15

HINDUISM ॐ

Hinduism is the oldest religion in the world. It is also the third largest religion with a following of about 900 million. No one really knows when Hinduism originated. This is mainly because the religion is a combination of various beliefs and traditions of ancient Indians. However, it is believed that the religion is at least 5000 years old! The followers of Hinduism are known as Hindus, most of whom live in India.

✠ *Unlike Vishnu and Shiva, Brahma the creator god is not widely worshipped by the Hindus*

THE TRINITY

Hindus believe in only one God. All the other gods are thought to be various forms of this Supreme Being. Of these forms, three are considered very important. They are Brahma, the creator, Vishnu, the preserver and Shiva, the destroyer of the Universe. Together they are known as the Trimurthi, or the Trinity. Vishnu is said to preserve life. Some Hindus believe that the Universe actually exists in Vishnu's dream and that it would be destroyed if he ever woke up. Some of the most popular gods of Hinduism, including Krishna and Rama, are incarnations of Vishnu. Another belief is that the Universe would be destroyed by Shiva, paving way for new creations.

DEVI

Goddesses play a very important role in Hinduism, and in fact, they are given more importance than even the gods. Hindus believe that the Supreme Being contains both male and female qualities and so worship the Supreme Goddess as Devi, or the Divine Mother. Devi is represented by her various forms – Lakshmi, Saraswati and Parvati.

✠ *Goddess Saraswati, one of the three forms of Devi, is worshipped as the goddess of knowledge and music*

OTHER GODS

Apart from Devi, the Trimurthi and various forms of Vishnu, Hindus also believe in thousands of lesser gods, or devas. These lesser gods are similar to angels and perform specific duties. For example, Indra, the lord of the devas, controls weather, while Agni controls fire. Varuna is the god of water and Yama is believed to be the god of death. Sons of gods like Ganesha and Karthikeya are also worshipped by the Hindus.

✠ *The elephant god, Ganesha, is one of the most popular gods. People worship him before the start of any new venture*

HINDU BELIEFS

THE HARMONY OF RELIGIONS
all true religions lead to the same goal – God

INCARNATION
whenever evil begins to rule the Earth,
God will take birth to restore the good

AHIMSA (non-violence)
we should not injure or kill any living being

SAMSARA
rebirth

KARMA
you shall reap as you sow; the deeds of the present life will determine whether a person will be re-incarnated or not

DHARMA
we should live a life of good morals and deeds
as explained in the scriptures

HUMANISM
All humans are equal, regardless of caste and colour

ATMAN
the soul is immortal and never changes

MOKSH
performing all duties with sincerity throughout the
various lifetimes will free the soul from the
endless cycle of birth and death

SACRED TEXTS

Upanishads: contains explanations about the basic beliefs of Hinduism
Bhagavat Gita: the "song of the Lord", is a part of the epic, Mahabharata. The Gita contains the words of Lord Krishna
Mahabharata: an epic poem that tells the story of conflict between the children of two brothers – Dhritharastra and Pandu – the two groups of warriors were Kauravas (Dhritharashtra's children) and Pandavas (Pandu's children)
Ramayana: the epic poem that deals with the life and times of Lord Rama, the great king of Ayodhya

✠ *Yagna, or yagya, an ancient Vedic ritual is still practised in India. In this ritual, Hindu priests make offerings to a particular god using Agni, or fire as a medium*

THE VEDAS

The principles of Hinduism have been explained in various scriptures, the most important being the Vedas. There are four Vedas – Rig Veda, Sama Veda, Yajur Veda and Atharva Veda. They are the oldest religious texts. It is believed that the Vedas were directly passed from God to scholars who then passed them on to the next generation by word of mouth. In ancient times, only people belonging to the Brahmin caste were allowed to learn the Vedas.

HINDU RITUALS AND FESTIVALS

The customs and traditions of Hindus are based on their religion. However, India is so vast that each custom varies according to the region. For example, the festival of Diwali, which is celebrated across India, has various legends attached to it. However, the main spirit behind the festival does not vary. Most Hindu festivals are seen as a celebration of the victory of good over evil.

FESTIVAL OF LIGHTS

Diwali, also known as the festival of lights, is one of the most important Hindu festivals. On this day, streets and homes are decorated with lamps. People wear new clothes, burst firecrackers and distribute sweets. In some states the festival is seen as a celebration of the return of Lord Rama to Ayodhya after killing the ten-headed demon, Ravana. Some consider it a celebration of the death of Narakasura at the hands of Krishna. Still others honour Lakshmi, the goddess of wealth, or Kali, the incarnation of Durga, on this day.

✛ In northern India, people offer prayers to both Lakshmi and Ganesha on Diwali

FESTIVAL OF COLOURS

Holi is another important Hindu festival. It is celebrated in the beginning of spring. It is called the festival of colours, as people smear each other with coloured powder, water or paint to celebrate it. On the night before Holi, people light bonfires to drive away evil. Holi is primarily a celebration of the eternal love between Lord Krishna and Radha. The festival also celebrates the death of the demoness, Holika.

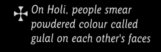

✛ On Holi, people smear powdered colour called gulal on each other's faces

OTHER MAJOR FESTIVALS

MAHASHIVARATRI
dedicated to Shiva

RAMA NAVAMI
birthday of Lord Rama

RAKSHA BANDHAN
celebrates the relationship between brothers and sisters

JANMASHTAMI
Lord Krishna's birthday

GANESH CHATURTHI
Lord Ganesha's birthday

HANUMAN JAYANTI
birthday of Hanuman, the monkey god

ONAM
Harvest festival of the state of Kerala

PONGAL
New Year of the state of Tamilnadu

This harvest festival is celebrated in the honour of goddess Durga, who killed Mahishasura, a terrible demon after fighting continuously for nine days and nine nights. The term Navaratri means "nine nights". The festival therefore lasts for nine nights. Many Hindus observe fast during these days. Hindus consider Navaratri an auspicious time to start new ventures. In some South Indian states Goddess Saraswati and Lord Ganesha are honoured on this day. Both deities are associated with knowledge, and therefore children conduct prayers for greater learning ability.

✠ The gods created Durga to slay Mahishasura. She possessed the combined powers of Vishnu, Shiva and Brahma, and all the lesser gods. She was also given the most powerful weapons of each god and a tiger to ride on

DASSERA

The tenth day following Navaratri is Vijay Dashami, more popularly known as Dass According to the epic, Ramayana, Lord R sought the blessing of Goddess Durga fc killing Ravana. Goddess Durga told Ram how he could slay the demon. Armed wit the knowledge, Rama killed Ravana on V Dashami and returned to Ayodhya with h Sita. Hindus celebrate this victory as Dass and burn dolls of Ravana, his son, Megh and brother Kumbhakaran at night.

✠ In the evening during Dassera, hundreds of people gather in open ground to burn the effigies of Ravana, Kumbhakaran and Meghnad

IMPORTANT RITUALS

Namakarana: naming ceremony
Niskraman: the child is taken out of the house for the first time, usually after three months
Annaprashana: feeding the child cereal for the first time, usually after six months
Chudakarma: shaving the head to remove impure hair, done between 1-3 years of age
Karnavedha: piercing the earlobes, between 3-5 years of age
Upanayan: Wearing of the sacred thread and beginning of studies
Vivaha: marriage
Antyeshti: Funeral

JAINISM

Jainism was founded in India over 2500 years ago. It is based on the teachings of Prince Mahavira, or Lord Mahavir (599-527 BC) as he is known to his followers who call themselves Jains. Today, there are about five million Jains all over the world.

TIRTHANKARAS

Jains believe in a chain of 24 leaders called Tirthankaras, who help people cross over from bad to good ways. Lord Mahavir is said to be the 24th or the last Tirthankara of this age. Mahavira was born into a royal family. He lived the life of a prince until, at the age of 30, he gave up his rich life. For the next 12 years, Mahavira led a strict and disciplined life. He hardly spoke and spent most of his time meditating. After attaining enlightenment, Mahavira travelled across the country preaching what he had learnt.

✝ *A statue of Lord Mahavira, the 24th Tirthankara, depicting the great saint in deep meditation*

THE WAY TO MOKSHA

Jains believe that the Universe is made up of jiva and ajiva or spiritual and non-spiritual matter. They believe that there are bits of jiva in all things from rocks, to plants, animals and even humans. Everything we do has a good or bad result called karma. Bad karma will weigh our jiva down just as good karma will lift it up. Jains think that karma causes us to be reborn again and again after our death. If we wish to get moksha or freedom from this cycle of birth and death then we must get rid of all karma.

THE FIVE PRINCIPLES

Ahimsa, or non-violence: do not injure any living creature.
Satya, or truth: never tell a lie
Asteya: never steal
Brahmacharya: refrain from sex if one is a monk or do not have sex outside marriage
Aparigrah: do not be obsessed with material things

AHIMSA AND THE JAIN DIET

Ahimsa is the most important principle of Jainism. It means avoiding injury to any living being. Some Jains take the principle of ahimsa to its extreme. They do not eat anything but fruits and vegetables. Some others do not eat vegetables which grow underground, like onions. Some Jains even wear masks over their mouth and nose to prevent breathing in any tiny insect and killing it.

✠ *A Svetambar monk in meditation*

✠ *The statue of Bahubali in Shravanabelagola in the South Indian state of Karnataka. Bahubali was the son of Rishabha, a king and the first Tirthankara. Bahubali gave up princely life to meditate and attain enlightenment. The statue depicts Bahubali during his penance*

JAIN SECTS

There are two types of Jains – Digambar and Svetambar. Digambar monks do not wear clothes, while Svetambar monks wear only white garments. Digambars believe that by not wearing clothes they are in fact not giving into their body's material needs. Another major difference between the two sects is that Svetambars allow nuns in their sect. Digambars believed that women could never attain moksha. However, this idea is changing and Digambar nuns are also becoming common.

NAMOKAR MANTRA

The chief Jain prayer

NAMO ARIHANTANAM
I bow to the Arahantas, the perfected human beings – Godmen

NAMO SIDDHANAM
I bow to the Siddhas, liberated bodiless souls – God

NAMO AARIYANAM
I bow to the Acharyas, the masters and heads of congregation

NAMO UVAJJHAYANAM
I bow to the Upadhyayas, the spiritual teacher

NAMO LOE SAVVA SAHUNAM
I bow to all the spiritual practitioners in the universe – Sadhus

ESO PANCH NAMOYARO
This fivefold prayer of worship

SAVVA PAVAPPANASANO
Destroys all sins and obstacles

MANGALANAM CHA SAVVESIN
And of all the holy chants

PADHAMAM HAVAI MANGALAM
Is the first and foremost

BUDDHISM

Buddhism is the fourth largest religion in the world, after Christianity, Islam and Hinduism. It was founded about 2,500 years ago in Nepal by a prince who gave up everything to discover the truth of life. Buddhism aims to teach its followers how to escape from the endless chain of birth and death.

A TROUBLED PRINCE

Siddhartha Gautama, the founder of Buddhism, was born a prince in Lumbini in present day Nepal. After his birth a seer foretold that he would be either a great king or a very holy man. Since his father the king was keen that Siddhartha succeed him, he took care to ensure that the young prince lived in the lap of luxury and was not shown anything that would turn him towards God. But, one day, in succession, Siddharth came across an old crippled man, a sick man, a decaying corpse, and finally a wandering holy man. This made him realise that life was full of pain and suffering from which there was no escape.

✝ *Siddhartha meditating to learn the truth of life. He later came to be known as the Buddha, or the "enlightened one".*

THE FOUR NOBLE TRUTHS

Dukkha: All worldly life is unsatisfactory and involves suffering
Samudaya: The cause of suffering is attachment or desire to worldly things
Nirodha: The end of suffering is attainment of Nirvana
Marga: There is a path that leads out of suffering, known as the Eightfold Path

IN SEARCH OF ANSWERS

Siddhartha left his wife, child and wealth and wandered in search of the means to escape the cycle of birth and death. After six years of study and meditation Siddhartha attained nirvana and got the answers he desired. He then spent the next 45 years spreading his knowledge and getting together a group of followers who would continue his work.

SPREAD OF BUDDHISM

Buddhism got its first royal support 200 years after it was founded when Emperor Ashoka of India became a Buddhist. He sent Buddhist missionaries to Sri Lanka and even faraway Syria. Today Budhism is Sri Lanka's main religion. About 1900 years ago Buddhism came to China. In the next 500 years, it spread to South East Asian countries like Thailand, Cambodia, Vietnam and Korea. In about 700 AD, Tibet was introduced to Buddhism and the head of the Tibetan Buddhists, the Dalai Lama, is perhaps the most famous Buddhist today. From China and Korea, Buddhism went to Japan. Today the majority of Japanese are Buddhists.

THE SCRIPTURES

The Buddhist scriptures are known as Tipitaka in Pali language, meaning "three baskets". This refers to the three main sections of the scriptures – Vinaya Pitaka, Sutta Pitaka and Abhidhamma Pitaka. Vinaya Pitaka consists of rules for the Sangha, or community of Buddhist monks and nuns. It also describes how these rules were instituted and the reasons behind it. The Sutta Pitaka contains the speeches of Buddha. The Abhidhamma Pitaka contains commentary on Buddhist principles and the teachings of Buddha.

✠ In Buddhism, a bodhisattva is a person who dedicates his life to help others achieve enlightenment. Kuan Yin, the Chinese goddess of mercy is a bodhisattva. She is known as Kannon in Japan and is a widely worshipped Buddhist deity

✠ The stupa at Sanchi in Madhya Pradesh, India was built by Ashoka and depicts the life of Gautama Buddha

THE EIGHTFOLD PATH

RIGHT UNDERSTANDING
RIGHT THOUGHT
RIGHT SPEECH
RIGHT ACTION
RIGHT LIVELIHOOD
RIGHT EFFORT
RIGHT MINDFULNESS
RIGHT CONCENTRATION

TAOISM

Taoism is less like a religion and more like a way of life. It is thought to have been started by Lao Tzu who worked as a librarian in the emperor's library about 2600 years ago in China. Tao means '*the way*.' Lao Tzu believed that if you want to be happy then you have to go with the flow.

THE BEGINNING OF TAOISM

Taoism, unlike other religions like Christianity and Islam, does not have one clear origin. It is a mix of various beliefs of the ancient Chinese. Taoism started as a philosophical thought promoted by wise men like Lao Tzu and Chuang Tse. It attained the form of a religion when it adapted certain principles of Chinese folk religion, especially shamanism and dualism (represented by the yin and yang). Shamans were an important part of ancient Chinese religion. They were men or women who could communicate with spirits and cure diseases. Taoism embraced these aspects of ancient Chinese life to become more acceptable to the common man.

TAOIST BELIEFS

The Tao created the universe
The Tao is the energy that flows through all life
The Tao surrounds everyone in nature
A Taoist aims to be one with the Tao
Everything in the universe is the Tao
The many gods are just versions of the one Tao
Everything is cyclical
Everybody must take care of their Tao through exercise and meditation
One should think before acting
People are born good
Follow the art of wu wei and let nature take it's course
Try not to be attached to anything material

✢ *Taoism embraced many aspects of Chinese folk religion including ancestral worship*

✢ *The Chinese character "Tao" means "way", or "path"*

THE BOOK OF TAO

According to legend, Lao Tzu was born as an 82 year old man. His name means, "Great Old Master" in Chinese. Towards the end of his life, Lao Tzu grew disillusioned with the constant wars and politics of the Emperor's court. He left his job and wandered through the wastelands. One day, as he was passing through the gate of the last outpost of the kingdom, a guard who had heard about his wisdom asked Lao Tzu to write it down. The book Lao Tzu wrote is called Tao Te Ching or the Book of the Way. This is regarded as the "bible" of Taoism.

TAOISM AS A RELIGION

Philosophical Taoism and religious Taoism are not very different from each other. However, religious Taoism relies heavily on supernatural beings like gods, demons and ancestral spirits. Meditation is vital to both, but it takes on the form of rituals and idol worship in religious Taoism. Ritualistic sacrifice, spiritual healing and ancestral worship – aspects that were not preached by Lao Tzu – are a big part of religious Taoism. Philosophical Taoism relies more on action through inaction (wu wei), emptiness, balance between the life forces and detachment from the material world.

YIN & YANG

Lao Tzu, like most Chinese of his time, believed that everything in the world was part of a universal life force. There were two sides to the life force, the yin and the yang. Yin is the dark side and yang the light side. Everyone has some yin and some yang in them, and Taoism says that it is important to keep both yin and yang balanced to attain harmony. Chinese doctors believed that a lot of illnesses were caused by too much yin or too much yang.

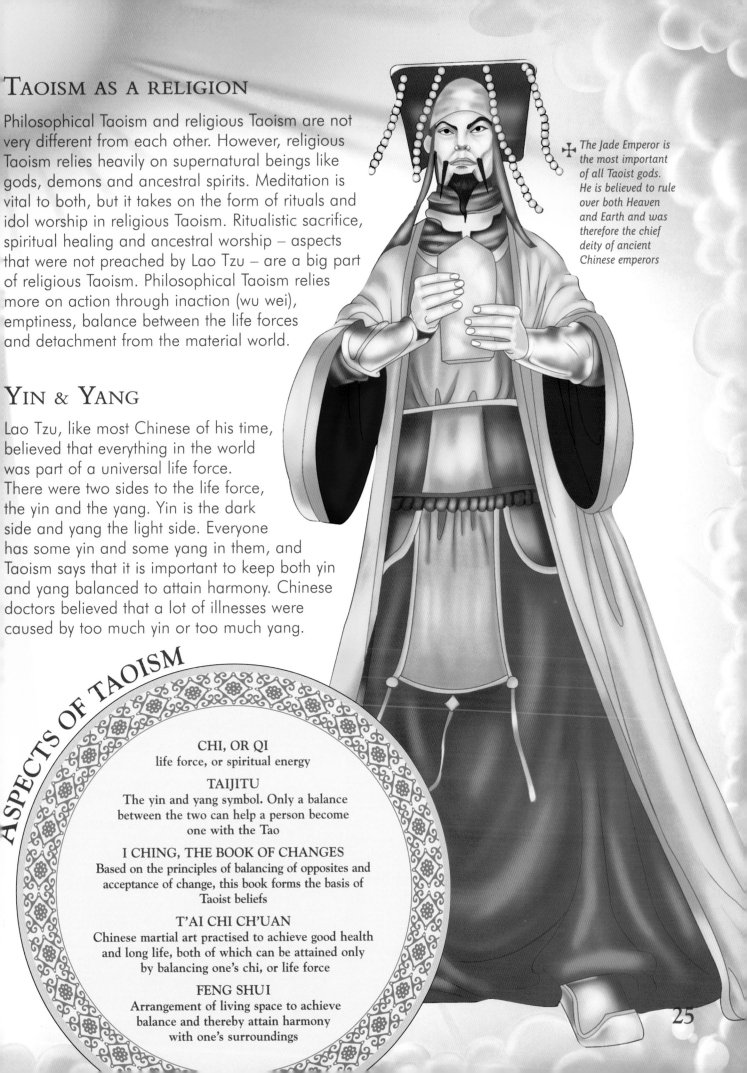

✞ The Jade Emperor is the most important of all Taoist gods. He is believed to rule over both Heaven and Earth and was therefore the chief deity of ancient Chinese emperors

ASPECTS OF TAOISM

CHI, OR QI
life force, or spiritual energy

TAIJITU
The yin and yang symbol. Only a balance between the two can help a person become one with the Tao

I CHING, THE BOOK OF CHANGES
Based on the principles of balancing of opposites and acceptance of change, this book forms the basis of Taoist beliefs

T'AI CHI CH'UAN
Chinese martial art practised to achieve good health and long life, both of which can be attained only by balancing one's chi, or life force

FENG SHUI
Arrangement of living space to achieve balance and thereby attain harmony with one's surroundings

25

CONFUCIANISM

Like Taoism, Confucianism also began as a philosophy. It was founded on the teachings of the famous Chinese philosopher, Confucius. This 2500-year-old Chinese religion does not believe in god! Confucianism is more a set of rules on how to live in a society. The rules are aimed particularly at leaders and people in high positions. They teach them how better to take care of and lead the people under them.

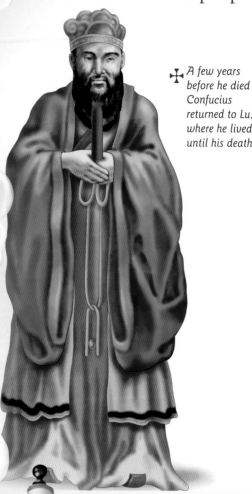

✝ *A few years before he died Confucius returned to Lu, where he lived until his death*

CONFUCIUS

Confucius was born into a once noble but poor family, but his parents managed to send him to school in the nearest big city. After his studies Confucius came back to his home city of Qufu in the State of Lu and took up a job as a teacher. Later he worked as a judge and then as the chief minister of Lu. Confucius did not much like the way the Duke of Lu was running affairs in his town. So he left his job and his town at the age of 50. For the rest of his life Confucius went from town to town with a few students advising the rulers how to be better at their jobs. Not everybody liked his advice and one even threw him in jail.

NOBILITY OF VIRTUE

In the old days people all over the world believed in class more than ability. They believed that a man born in a rich family was better than one born in a poor family, even if the poor man had more talent. Confucius sought to change this belief. He said a commoner who cultivated good habits could be called a gentleman. At the same time an ill-mannered prince was just a small man. As more people began to follow Confucianism, they put in place ways like examinations, through which a poor but talented person could still rise to a high position in society. Today, this way of choosing the brightest people for the top jobs in government is followed all over the world.

THE FOUR BOOKS CONFUCIANISM

The Great Learning: a chapter in the Classic of Rites and an introduction to Confucianism
The Doctrine of the Mean: a chapter in the Classic of Rites supposedly written by Kong Ji, the grandson of Confucius
The Analects of Confucius: a book of sayings by Confucius said to be recorded by his followers
The Mencius: a book of discussions between the famous Confucian, Mencius, and the kings of his time

Shi Huangdi, the founder of the Qin dynasty ordered the burning of books so that his people would not have enough knowledge to question his rule

EARLY SUPPRESSION

The ideas of Confucius were not accepted during his lifetime. In fact, Confucianism did not find many followers until the Han dynasty. Even then, followers did not have direct access to his ideas, as most of his books were destroyed during the Book Burning movement of the Qin Dynasty. The Analects of Confucius is the only existing document that contains the actual words spoken by the great philosopher. Everything else is an interpretation by later followers.

NEO-CONFUCIANISM

After its revival during the period of the Han Dynasty, Confucianism became the official state religion. However, Confucianism lacked a clear structure and was too complicated for the common man, who preferred the simple principles of Taoism and Buddhism. This led to the emergence of Neo-Confucianism, which incorporated some Taoist and Buddhist ideas with Confucianism. However, Neo-Confucians continued to oppose Buddhism and Taoism as a whole.

Confucianism got its religious tones only after it adopted certain Taoist and Buddhist rituals like burning of incense sticks during prayers

CONFUCIAN VALUES

LI
describes rules of good behaviour in society

HSIAO
love and respect within the family; respect for one's elders, including employers and rulers

XIN
trustworthiness and honesty

YI
righteousness

JEN
show kindness to all and not do anything that you would not like done to yourself

CHUNG
loyalty to the state

JUNZI
the perfect gentleman, who follows the Confucian values

SHINTO

Shinto is the native religion of Japan. Until the end of World War II it was the state religion. Shinto promotes the worship of spirits of nature and of dead ancestors. Nobody knows when Shinto began because the Japanese only had a written language from about 1500 years ago and Shinto was already in existence much before that.

ORIGINS

It is difficult to say when the religion actually took shape. However, it is widely believed that Shinto was already in existence during the Jomon period (10,000-300 BC). Scientists believe that the islands of Japan were once connected to the mainland by ice. People from eastern and south-eastern Asia are thought to have walked over these glaciers and settled as separate tribes in Japan. Each tribe probably had its own set of gods and rituals. Over the years, these folk religions might have come together, with the gods of the imperial family gaining importance over the others. The religion itself did not have a name until the introduction of Buddhism. Shinto is commonly translated as "the Way of the Gods".

✠ *A typical shinto shrine in Japan*

✠ *A Shinto Shrine and its surrounding area are referred to as jinja*

KAMI

Shinto gods are called Kami. In Shinto there are more than eight million of them! The most widely worshipped kami is Amaterasu the sun-goddess. Her main shrine or temple is at Ise in Japan. She is often symbolised by a mirror in her shrines.

IMPORTANT SHINTO SHRINES

Ise Shrine, Ise: shrine of Amaterasu
Atsuta Shrine in Nagoya, Aichi: shrine of the Imperial sword, Kusanagi
Heian Jingu, Kyoto: shrine of Japanese Emperors Kammu and Komei
Meiji Shrine: dedicated to Emperor Meiji

TYPES OF SHINTO

Shinto has been divided into four different types, each of which focuses on different aspects of Shinto. *Shrine Shinto* is the oldest of these. People who follow this Shinto type, worship in shrines. *Sect Shinto* is a fairly recent form of Shinto where people conduct religious activities in meeting halls. There are different Shinto sects like mountain-worship sects (who worship mountains), faith-healing sects, and Confucian sects. *Folk Shinto* is a mix of ancient Shinto beliefs with bits of Taoism, Confucianism and Buddhism mixed in. *State Shinto* was the official religion in Japan until the end of World War II. It laid emphasis on worshipping the Emperor. After Japan's defeat in the war, State Shinto ended and the emperor had to announce that he was no longer god.

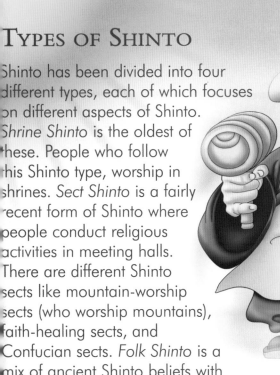

✝ *Followers of Shinto believe in the Shichi-fuku-jin, or the Seven Gods of Luck. Of these, Daikokuten, the god of wealth and Ebisu, the god of fishermen and merchants are often depicted together as they are believed to be father and son*

EMA

Long ago rich people would donate horses to shrines when they wished for a large favour from the gods. For smaller favours they would often just donate a picture of a horse on a wooden tablet. These tablets are called ema. People hang them up inside the shrine in the hope that their wish will be granted.

✝ *Today, outside most Shinto shrines you can buy ema with different pictures on them*

FOUR AFFIRMATIONS

TRADITION AND THE FAMILY
The family is very important in Shinto. All the main celebrations relate to birth and marriage

LOVE OF NATURE
Shintoists believe that to be close to nature is to be close to the Kami

PHYSICAL CLEANLINESS
Shintoists take baths, wash their hands, and rinse their mouth often

MATSURI
This is any festival dedicated to the Kami, and there are many all round the year

CHRISTIANITY ✝

Christianity is the world's largest religion with about 2.1 billion adherents from all countries of the world. Its origins, as Judaism and Islam, can be traced back to Abraham. Christians believe that Jesus Christ is the Messiah sent by God to pay the price of their sins and lead them to heaven.

SON OF GOD

Christianity originated over two thousand years ago as a reformed branch of Judaism. Both religions believe in the early religious figures such as Adam, Noah, Abraham, Jacob and Moses. However, the main difference between the two religions is that Christians believe in Jesus Christ. They believe that God revealed himself through his son, Jesus. They believe that Jesus came to earth to teach about love and brotherhood, and that he died on the cross to pay for the sins of mankind.

THE BIRTH OF JESUS

Jesus is said to have been born in Bethlehem to Mary and her husband Joseph, a humble carpenter. Joseph and Mary were forced to leave their home in Nazareth to return to Joseph's homeland, Bethlehem for a census. When they arrived in Bethlehem they had no place to stay. Finally the couple were given a stable for the night. It was in this stable that Baby Jesus was born in a manger.

THE TWELVE DISCIPLES OF JESUS

Simon (called Peter)
Andrew (Peter's brother)
James (son of Zebedee)
John (brother of James)
Philip (from Bethsaida)
Bartholomew (also Nathaniel)
Thomas (also called Didymus)
Matthew (a tax collector)
James (son of Alphaeus)
Thaddaeus (or Judas, brother of James)
Simon (the Zealot or Canaanite)
Judas Iscariot

✠ *The nativity scene depicting the birth of Jesus is one of the most popular images of Christianity*

LIFE OF JESUS

Jesus grew up in Nazareth and became a carpenter like his father. At the age of 30, Jesus was baptised by John the Baptist who recognised Jesus as the Messiah, the Son of God. He then went into wilderness for 40 days and asked for guidance. He then began his teaching and performed his first miracle at a wedding in Cana. When the hosts ran out of wine, Jesus came to their rescue by changing water into wine. Jesus went on to perform many more miracles and gained many loyal followers including his twelve disciples. His increasing popularity earned him the wrath of the Jewish leaders and the Romans who captured him with the help of his treacherous disciple Judas Iscariot. Jesus was tried and sentenced to death. He was crucified on a wooden cross, which has become the symbol of Christianity. Christians believe that Jesus rose from the dead after three days and is now in Heaven waiting to come again on the day of judgement.

OTHER MIRACLES OF JESUS

Cures a royal official's son at Capernaum

Cures Peter's mother-in-law

Calms a storm at sea

Walks on water

A woman with haemorrhage is healed after she touches Jesus' robe

Feeds 5000 with just five loaves of bread and two fish

Restores sight to a blind man at Bethsaida

Raises Lazarus from the dead

Heals ten lepers

THE HOLY BIBLE

The holy book of Christians is called the Holy Bible. It is a collection of books written by different people over a very long period of time. The Holy Bible is made up of the Old and the New Testaments. The Old Testament is very similar to the Jewish Bible from which it is derived. The Old Testament generally has 39 books but the Catholic version of the Old Testament has four more books. The New Testament has 27 books, which tell the story of Jesus and his message.

The New Testament of the Holy Bible was primarily

MANY FORMS OF CHRISTIANITY

For almost a thousand years the Catholic Church was the only denomination in Christianity. The Orthodox Christians split with the Catholic Church in 1054. Later in the 16th century the Protestants also went their own way. Today there are many other denominations within Christianity. However, all Christians share common beliefs.

CATHOLIC

Catholicism is the largest denomination in Christianity. There are about 1.1 billion Catholics in the world. Catholics believe that the Pope, based in Rome, is the successor to Saint Peter whom Christ appointed as the first head of his church. Catholicism is different from other Christian churches in both its organisation and in its teaching. The Catholic faith revolves around the seven sacraments, at least four of which are compulsory for every grown up Catholic. Although Catholicism was once very popular in Europe and the USA, it has lost its influence in recent years. However, the number of Catholics in Africa and Asia is increasing steadily.

✝ *Catholics regard the Pope as Christ's representative on Earth*

✝ *Orthodox churches can be identified by their colourful domes*

ORTHODOX

Orthodox means right thinking in Greek. The Orthodox Church follows the teachings of Christ with as little change as possible. The Bible of the Orthodox Church is the same as that of the Western churches except that it is not based on the version written in Hebrew, but on an ancient Greek translation called the Septuagint. The Orthodox churches are based in Greece, Eastern Europe and parts of Middle East and Africa.

PROTESTANT

In the 16th century there was a movement in Europe to change the practices of the Catholic Church. It was called the Reformation. The Protestant churches grew out of the Reformation. The origin of Protestantism is connected with the issues raised by Martin Luther, a famous Augustinian monk. Martin Luther, who denied papal authority after becoming disillusioned with the Catholic Church, proposed many reforms. Luther's reforms found widespread acceptance within no time.

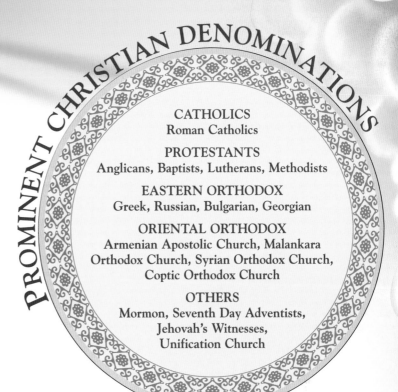

PROMINENT CHRISTIAN DENOMINATIONS

CATHOLICS
Roman Catholics

PROTESTANTS
Anglicans, Baptists, Lutherans, Methodists

EASTERN ORTHODOX
Greek, Russian, Bulgarian, Georgian

ORIENTAL ORTHODOX
Armenian Apostolic Church, Malankara Orthodox Church, Syrian Orthodox Church, Coptic Orthodox Church

OTHERS
Mormon, Seventh Day Adventists, Jehovah's Witnesses, Unification Church

THE FIVE SOLAS OF PROTESTANTISM

Sola fide: by faith alone, meaning only faith can make one guiltless before God

Sola scriptura: by scripture alone, meaning the Bible is the only authoritative Word of God, and everyone can interpret it

Solus Christus: Christ alone, meaning only Christ can mediate between God and man

Sola gratia: by grace alone, meaning salvation can be attained only by grace and not merit

Soli Deo gloria: glory to God alone – Protestants believe that people like saints and popes were not worthy of the glory given to them

MORMON

"Mormon" refers to the followers of the Church of Jesus Christ of Latter-day Saints. Mormons believe that after the death of Jesus Christ and the twelve apostles, the Church that Christ had established became influenced by pagan religions and spiritual leaders began to stray from the original teachings of Christ. To restore the lost glory, God and Jesus appeared to a 14-year old boy named Joseph Smith Jr. and made him the first prophet of the restored church. Ten years later, Joseph Smith Jr. established the Church of Jesus Christ of Latter-day Saints in Fayette, New York.

CELEBRATING JESUS

Christian festivals revolve around events in Christ's life and the lives of the various saints. Some celebrations such as the harvest festival are, however, very ancient festivals, which have been brought into the Christian year.

ADVENT

Advent is a period during which Christians prepare themselves to celebrate the birth of Christ. It begins with the Sunday nearest to 30 November and lasts for four Sundays until Christmas. So, Advent may last from 21–28 days. The religious year of the Church begins with Advent. Advent is also a reminder of the Second Coming of Jesus.

✠ *The lighting of the candles on the Advent wreath is the most important ritual of Advent*

OTHER FESTIVALS

Ascension Day
Pentecost
Epiphany
St. Patrick's Day
St. Joseph's Feast
Feast of the Assumption
All Souls' Day
St. Andrew's Day
Trinity Sunday
Ash Wednesday
Harvest Festival

CHRISTMAS

Christmas is the most important Christian festival after Easter, Pentecost and Epiphany, but it is undoubtedly the most popular. Traditionally, Christmas is celebrated over a 12 day period which begins on December 25 – the birthday of Christ – and ends with the Feast of the Epiphany on January 6.

✠ *Decorating the Christmas tree with ornaments and lights has now become one of the most popular Christmas traditions*

LENT

The forty days (not counting Sundays) before Easter are known as Lent, which remembers the time Jesus spent in the wilderness. During Lent, Christians give up bad habits and prepare themselves spiritually for Easter. Lent begins on Ash Wednesday and ends on Holy Saturday, the day before Easter. The last week of Lent is called the Holy Week. It begins with Palm Sunday which remembers Jesus' entrance into Jerusalem.

Important days in Holy Week are Maundy Thursday which commemorates Christ's last supper and his betrayal by Judas, and Good Friday, on which day Christians remember Jesus' arrest, trial and death.

✝ On Palm Sunday, people carrying palm fronds or wooden crosses enter the church symbolising the entry of Jesus into Jerusalem

THE SEVEN SACRAMENTS

Orthodox Christians and Roman Catholics believe in the following seven sacraments, or mysteries:

Baptism: cleansing of sins with Holy water

Communion: a rite performed in the memory of Jesus who gave his disciples bread and wine at the Last Supper saying it was his body and blood

Marriage: considered to be an inseparable bond between a man and a woman

Holy Orders: the orders of the bishop, priest and deacon

Confirmation: a statement of faith by a mature, baptised person who fully understands the ways of God

Penance: the method by which a baptised person can confess his sins to a priest and obtain forgiveness of the Lord by repenting in earnest

Anointing of the sick: the rite in which a priest blesses a person seriously ill with holy oil

EASTER

Easter is Christianity's main festival. It celebrates Christ's resurrection, or rising from the dead. The season of Easter lasts for fifty days until the Pentecost. Easter is a moveable feast because it never falls on the same day each year. Easter is often celebrated by an Easter vigil, which is a special service held at midnight, when Christ is thought to have risen from the dead. Easter eggs are given as gifts because eggs represent new life.

✝ Easter bunny and Easter eggs are the most popular symbols of Easter

35

ISLAM

Islam is the world's largest religion after Christianity. It has over a billion followers, who are known as Muslims. The word 'Islam' has its roots in the Arabic word *silm*, meaning 'to surrender in peace.' Islam stands for the complete and peaceful surrender of man to the will of Allah, or God. Islam is believed to have originated in the 7th century in the cities of Mecca and Medina, both in present-day Saudi Arabia.

✚ *Islamic art is a combination of geometric designs, calligraphy and floral patterns*

COMMON ANCESTOR

Just like Christianity and Judaism, Islam is an Abrahamic religion as well. In fact, many Islamic beliefs are similar to that of Jews and Christians. Abraham is known as Ibrahim to Muslims. Muslims are believed to be descendants of Ishmael, Ibrahim's son by his second wife, Hagar.

✚ *Islamic prayer beads are called tasbih or subah. They have 99 beads used to call out the 99 names of Allah*

THE LAST PROPHET

Once, a merchant named Muhammad bin Abdullah was meditating in a cave near Mecca. The angel Gabriel came to him and told him that Allah had chosen him as the last prophet on Earth. The angel asked Muhammad to memorise verses that were later collected as the Koran, the holy book of the Muslims. The merchant set about spreading the message of Allah and, in time, came to be regarded as the founder of Islam.

SACRED TEXTS

Hadith: a set of books that contains the sayings of Prophet Muhammad

Sira: Biography of Prophet Muhammad

Fiqh: The legal views of Islamic lawmakers

Sharia: Set of Islamic laws that governs both religious and day-to-day life

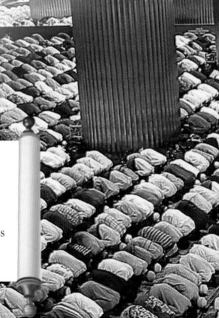

THE TEACHINGS OF MUHAMMAD

The Koran is believed to contain the true message of Allah as revealed to Muhammad by the angel Gabriel. These revelations were made to the prophet on separate occasions, probably over a period of 20 years, and later were spread among the people by Muhammad and his followers. They were compiled into a single book several years after Muhammad's death in 632. The Koran comprises 114 surat, or chapters, and includes several stories from the Bible as well. The book also recognises Jesus Christ as a great prophet. For followers of Islam, the Koran is the final source of authority on all matters, be it religious or political.

✣ *The salah is done facing towards the Kabah shrine in Mecca*

ISLAMIC SECTS

Islam has many sects. The main ones are Sunni and Shia. Sunnites claimed that Muhammad died without a successor. Later, Muhammad's followers chose Abu Bakr, the prophet's father-in-law and close friend, as the first *caliph*. On the other hand, Shia Muslims held that Muhammad appointed his son-in-law Ali ibn Abi Talib as his successor and the first *imam*.

THE FIVE PILLARS

SHAHADAH
Allah is the only God and Muhammad is his messenger

SALAH
The five daily prayers

ZAKAT
All Muslims must give a part of their income in charity

RAMADAN
Fasting from dawn to dusk everyday through the month of Ramadan

HAJJ
All Muslims have to visit Mecca during the month of Dhul Hijjah, at least once in their lifetime

TEST OF FAITH

A few main holidays are common to Muslims all over the globe. These are the Islamic New Year which is celebrated on the first day of the month of Muharram; Ashura, a day of fasting kept on the 10th day of Muharram; Eid ul-Adha; Mawlid an-Nabi; Isra Mer'Aj; Ramadan and Eid ul-Fitr.

✝ *During Ramadan, Muslims usually gather together to break their fast in the evenings. The evening meal is referred to as iftar, which mean "break fast" in Arabic*

RAMADAN

Ramadan is the ninth month of the Islamic calendar. It was in this month that the Koran was revealed by God to Prophet Muhammad. Devout Muslims keep a month long fast during Ramadan. Fasting Muslims do not eat or drink anything from sunrise to sunset. They also do not smoke during this month. At sunset the fast is broken with a prayer and a light meal of fruits called the iftar. They wake up very early the next morning and have a breakfast before sunrise and then resume the fast.

EID UL-FITR

Muslims celebrate the end of a month of fasting during the month of Ramadan with Eid ul-Fitr. On this day, all Muslims put on new clothes and go to the nearest mosque for the special Eid service. Afterwards, families visit their friends and share Eid greetings. It is also a day for feasting. In some countries children receive gifts, or money. Nowadays, many Muslims send Eid ul-Fitr cards to their friends and relatives.

EID UL-ADHA

Muslims remember Abraham's readiness to sacrifice his son to God by celebrating Eid ul-Adha. The most important part of the celebration is the animal sacrifice. Most families slaughter a sheep or maybe even a cow or camel, and share the meat with neighbours, relatives and the poor. The animal to be slaughtered must be *halal*, or fit for sacrifice. Eid ul-Adha is celebrated after the end of the Hajj, the annual pilgrimage to Mecca, about 70 days after Eid ul-Fitr. Unlike Eid ul-Fitr, which is a one day feast, Eid ul-Adha lasts for four days.

MUHARRAM

The festival of Muharram is an important event for Shia Muslims. Through this festival they remember the death of Husayn bin Ali, a grandson of Prophet Muhammad. The faithful take out processions chanting "Ya Husayn" and beating their chests as a sign of sorrow. They also gather to watch enactments of Husayn's death and listen to sad poems about him.

ISLAMIC MONTHS

Muharram	Safar
Rabi`-ul-Awwal	Rabi`-ul-Akhir
Jumaada-ul-Awwal	Jumaada-ul-Akhir
Rajab	Sha'aban
Ramadan	Shawwal
Dhul Qadah	Dhul Hijjah

SIX ARTICLES OF BELIEF

Common to all Muslims:

Belief in God,
the one and only one worthy
of all worship

Belief in all the Prophets and Messengers
sent by God

Belief in the Books sent by God

Belief in the Angels

Belief in the Day of Judgment
and in the Resurrection

Belief in Destiny

✠ *Animal sacrifices form a major part of the Eid ul-Adha celebrations*

39

SIKHISM ੴ

Sikhism was founded in the early fifteenth century by an Indian teacher called Guru Nanak. This great teacher taught that all people were born equal and that religion should not divide them. He travelled far and wide urging people to stop following empty rituals. He was succeeded by nine other gurus one after the other. There are over 25 million Sikhs worldwide.

GURU NANAK

Guru Nanak was born in a village called Talwandi, near Lahore in present-day Pakistan. He led a normal life until one day at the age of 28, he went bathing in the nearby river. He was gone three days. When he came back, Guru Nanak declared that God was the same, no matter which religion you followed. Guru Nanak spent the rest of his life travelling and spreading his teachings. He went all over India and as far as Sri Lanka, Mecca and Baghdad. He spent the last 15 years of his life in a village called Kartapur in Punjab, India. It was while he was here that his followers first began to call themselves Sikhs, or disciples.

SIKH BELIEFS

Sikhs believe that there is only one God. They believe that God has always existed and always will exist and that He created the Universe. They also believe that God has no shape or gender, and that He has never come and will never come to earth in human form. Sikhs believe that God never hates and is not afraid of anyone and that He only speaks the truth. According to Sikhs, God reaches out to us through his words, which are passed on by the Gurus, and laid down in the form of shabads, or hymns used in Sikh worship.

✠ *The gold and silver palki, or palanquin, which holds the Guru Granth Sahib at the Golden Temple, Amritsar. On Guru Nanak's birthday, this palki is taken out in a procession*

THE ELEVENTH GURU

The Guru Granth Sahib, the Holy Book of the Sikhs, is considered the eleventh guru of the religion. Sikhs believe the Granth to be their Eternal Guru. The book was made by Guru Gobind Singh, the tenth guru. The Granth contains 1430 pages dedicated to the actual teachings of the ten gurus and teachers of other religions.

✛ *During festivals, marriages and other occasions, Sikhs conduct Akhand path, in which the Granth Sahib is read continuously for two days*

THE TEN GURUS

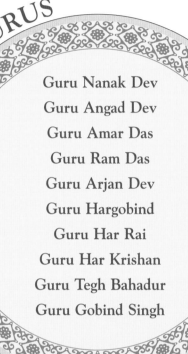

Guru Nanak Dev

Guru Angad Dev

Guru Amar Das

Guru Ram Das

Guru Arjan Dev

Guru Hargobind

Guru Har Rai

Guru Har Krishan

Guru Tegh Bahadur

Guru Gobind Singh

THE FIVE Ks

Kesh (uncut hair): a Sikh never cuts or trims hair

Khanga (comb): Sikhs wear a small comb in their hair all the time

Karra (circular bracelet): this is worn on the right hand if one is a right hander or else on the left

Kachera (shorts): a pair of knee length shorts generally worn as underwear

Kirpan (sword): a small curved sword

THE KHALSA

The word "Khalsa" means pure in Punjabi. In Sikhism, a Khalsa is one who has been baptised through the Amrit Sanskar. This ceremony was first performed by Guru Gobind Singh. It involves drinking of Amrit, or holy sugar water stirred with a dagger, in the presence of the Granth and five Khalsa Sikhs. A Khalsa Sikh is one who has surrendered himself or herself to the will of God and is therefore expected to lead a disciplined life and strictly follow the teachings of the gurus. Khalsa Sikhs can be identified by the five Ks that they carry on them always.

✛ *Guru Gobind Singh performed the first ever Amrit Sanskar in 1699 on the day of the Baisakhi, the spring festival. Sikhs celebrate Baisakhi by taking out processions, offering prayers at gurudwaras and with music and Bhangra, a folk dance*

41

BAHA'I

Baha'i-ism is the youngest of the world's religions. It is also one of the fastest growing religions. It uses the best teachings from the major religions of the world and believes that mankind is all one and should live in unity. The religion was founded by Mírzá Husayn-'Alí who lived in Iran.

BAB & BAHA'U'LLAH

Siyyid Mírzá 'Alí-Muhammad was born in Shiraz in 1819. In 1844 he declared that he was the prophet of God that some Muslims were expecting. He began to attract many followers but angered most Muslims who believed that Muhammad was the last prophet and that there could be none after him. The Bab, as Ali-Muhammad was now called, was arrested and executed by a firing squad in 1850. Thirteen years later Mírzá Husayn-'Alí, a follower of the Bab declared himself the messenger of God that the Bab had talked about and began to use the title of Baha'u'llah or Glory of God.

BAHA'I HOUSES OF WORSHIP

Baha'is do not have temples in each town and usually meet in homes or meeting halls. They do, however, have seven Houses of Worship around the world. All Houses of Worship look different from each other but have two things in common. They all have nine sides and are topped by a dome. The first House of Worship was built in 1908, in Ashkhabad, Turkmenistan, but it no longer stands. The oldest House of Worship still in use is in Wilmette, Illinois, USA and was built in 1953. Apart from this, Houses of Worship also exist in Kampala, Uganda; Sydney, Australia; Langenhain, Germany; Panama City, Panama; Tiapapata, Western Samoa and in New Delhi, India.

The Universal House of Justice at Haifa, Israel, is responsible for applying the laws of the faith and the growth of the Baha'i community

✠ *The Lotus Temple in New Delhi, India, is one of the famous Bahá'í houses of worship*

HOLY DAYS OF BAHA'IS

Baha'is observe 11 holy days, nine of which are major. Bahai's do not work on major holy days. They celebrate the holy days by organising prayer services. Of the nine major holy days, the Ridvan Festival is the Most Great Festival. It commemorates Baha'u'llah's announcment that he was the prophet the Bab had promised. This was done in the garden of Ridvan. The festival is celebrated from 21st April to 2nd May. The first, ninth and the twelfth days are considered major holy days. They commemorate the arrival of Baha'u'llah at the Ridvan garden, the arrival of his family and their departure from Ridvan.

MAJOR HOLY DAYS

Naw-Ruz: Baha'i New Year celebrated on 21st March

Nineteen Day Feast: Every nineteen days all Baha'is in a community meet at one of the houses or the local meeting hall to celebrate the beginning of a Baha'i month

Declaration of the Bab: celebrated from 22-23 May in memory of the day the Bab declared to the world about the coming of Baha'u'llah

Ascension of Baha'u'llah: death anniversary of Baha'u'llah observed on 29th May

Martyrdom of the Bab: death anniversary of the Bab observed on 9th July

Birth of the Bab: major holy day celebrated on 20th October

Birth of Baha'u'llah: celebrated on 12th November

✠ *The Shrine of the Bab in Haifa, Israel, where the Bab is buried is an important Baha'i pilgrimage*

BAHA'I RITUALS

Baha'is have no priest or nuns. They have no sacraments like Christians and they have just three rituals. All Baha'is say daily prayers. Baha'is have a special prayer for the dead, which is recited at a funeral. Baha'is also have a simple marriage rite. Other than these, the Baha'is do not follow any traditional or ritualistic ceremony, as they believe that such ceremonies lose meaning when people forget the spiritual purpose behind them.

✠ *Different lists are sometimes found but this embodies the main points*

THE TWELVE SOCIAL PRINCIPLES

The Oneness of God
The Oneness of religion
The Oneness of mankind
Equality of men and women
Elimination of all forms of prejudice
World peace kept by a world body
Harmony of religion and science
Universal compulsory education
Obedience to government and non-involvement in politics
Independent investigation of truth
The need for a universal auxiliary language
Elimination of extremes of wealth and poverty and a spiritual solution to economic problems

FAMOUS PLACES OF WORSHIP

From the very beginning, all over the world, some of the finest buildings have been houses of worship. Man has always given his best to God. Places of worship are also built to last a long time, much longer than the average house. They are also built to accommodate a lot of people.

ST. PETER'S BASILICA

The Basilica of Saint Peter is the largest church in the world. It can seat 60,000 people! It is built on the place where St. Peter, the first Pope is buried. The basilica that stands today was built over a period of 120 years in the 16th and 17th centuries. The basilica before that had been built by the Roman emperor Constantine and had stood for 1200 years. Many Popes, including the last one, are also buried in St. Peter's Basilica.

✠ *The dome of St. Peter's Basilica was designed by the famous Renaissance sculptor and painter, Michelangelo, but was completed only after his death by the Italian architect Giacomo della Porta*

MASJID AL HARAM

The Masjid al Haram is a mosque in the city of Mecca. Muslims consider it to be the most sacred spot on Earth. Every year tens of thousands of Muslims make a pilgrimage to the Masjid al Haram as part of the hajj. Muslims believe that the mosque was built by Abraham and his son Ishmael. In the centre of the mosque's inner courtyard is a square structure called the Kaaba which Muslims believe is modelled on God's house in heaven. The mosque as it exists today has a grand marble façade and three stories. Each storey can accommodate thousands of the faithful.

✠ *The cornerstone on the fourth corner of the Kaaba is believed to have fallen from Heaven and is called the Black Stone. According to Muslims, the stone turned black because of man's sins*

Sri Venkateswara Temple

The Sri Venkateswara Hindu temple stands atop the holy hill of Tirumala in Andhra Pradesh, India. More people visit it than any other religious site in the world. Unlike most Hindu temples, entry to the Sri Venkateswara temple is open to people of all religions. The popularity of this temple means that it is also the richest temple in India. The main festival at this temple is the nine day Brahmotsavam festival held in September or October. During the festival the temple is decorated, special pujas held and colourful chariot processions taken out.

✠ *More than 50,000 devotees visit the Sri Venkateswara Temple every day. About 19 million visitors have been recorded in a year. It is believed that the idol of Lord Venkateswara was formed naturally and not sculpted by anyone*

Chionin Temple

Chionin is the head temple of the Jodo or Pure Land sect of Japanese Buddhism. The Jodo sect was founded by Honen in 1175. It is one of the largest Buddhist sects in Japan today because its teachings are much simpler than other Buddhists sects. Chionin was first built in 1234, but the original building no longer exists. The oldest buildings still standing in the temple complex were built in the 17th century. The Sanmon gate of the Chionin temple is Japan's largest temple gate. The temple also has the country's largest bell.

✠ *The Chionin Temple is located in Kyoto, Japan*

Golden Temple

The Golden Temple in Amritsar, Punjab is the holiest Sikh temple. It is also called the Harmandir Sahib. It was built between 1588 and 1601 on land gifted by the Mughal emperor Akbar. The temple has a gold dome and is decorated with a lot of gold and marble. Most of the precious decorations were paid for by Maharaja Ranjit Singh who was a Sikh.

✠ *The foundation stone for the Golden Temple was laid by a Muslim saint, Hazrat Mian Mir*

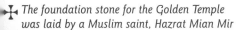

45